WINDOWS OF THE HEART

POETIC MUSINGS ON LOVE, LOSS, AND THE BEAUTY OF NIGHT

SATYAM RANJAN

Copyright © Satyam Ranjan
All Rights Reserved.

This book has been self-published with all reasonable efforts taken to make the material error-free by the author. No part of this book shall be used, reproduced in any manner whatsoever without written permission from the author, except in the case of brief quotations embodied in critical articles and reviews.

The Author of this book is solely responsible and liable for its content including but not limited to the views, representations, descriptions, statements, information, opinions and references ["Content"]. The Content of this book shall not constitute or be construed or deemed to reflect the opinion or expression of the Publisher or Editor. Neither the Publisher nor Editor endorse or approve the Content of this book or guarantee the reliability, accuracy or completeness of the Content published herein and do not make any representations or warranties of any kind, express or implied, including but not limited to the implied warranties of merchantability, fitness for a particular purpose. The Publisher and Editor shall not be liable whatsoever for any errors, omissions, whether such errors or omissions result from negligence, accident, or any other cause or claims for loss or damages of any kind, including without limitation, indirect or consequential loss or damage arising out of use, inability to use, or about the reliability, accuracy or sufficiency of the information contained in this book.

Made with ❤ on the Notion Press Platform
www.notionpress.com

This book contains a special dedication to my grandfather, Late Shri NKP Singh. Through one poem, I pay homage to his wise, kind, and loving spirit that has left a lasting impact on my life and the lives of many others. May his memory continue to inspire and guide us, always

"In loving memory of my grandfather Late Shri NKP Singh, whose gentle touch and kind heart left a lasting imprint on our lives, reminding us that the greatest legacy we can leave is a trail of love and kindness in this world."

MY GRANDFATHER AND ME JUST AFTER BATH

Contents

Foreword

As you embark on this literary journey, I am honored to introduce you to a collection of thought-provoking and insightful reflections by the author. The poems in this book delve into the complexities of human emotions, experiences, and relationships, offering a window into the author's world and an invitation for introspection.

Throughout these pages, you will find expressions of love, loss, hope, and self-discovery, all woven together with the author's unique voice and style. The words are at once personal and universal, evoking feelings that are familiar to us all.

As you read this book, I hope you find moments of inspiration, comfort, and understanding. Whether you are a seasoned reader or a newcomer to the world of poetry, I am confident that you will find something of value in these pages.

So, sit back, relax, and allow yourself to be transported to a world where words have the power to evoke deep emotions, spark new perspectives, and leave a lasting impact on your soul.

Enjoy the journey!

Preface

It is my great pleasure to present this book of poetry to you, the reader. These poems are a manifestation of my thoughts, feelings, and experiences, captured in verse and offered as a gift to you.

As you read through these pages, you will discover a tapestry of emotions, from the joys of love and the peace of contentment to the heartache of loss and the struggles of self-discovery. The poems in this book delve into the human experience, exploring the complexities of our relationships, our relationships with the world around us, and our relationship with ourselves.

Writing these poems has been a journey of self-expression and introspection for me, and I hope that they will touch your heart and spark meaningful conversations for you as well. Whether you are an avid reader of poetry or a newcomer to the genre, I invite you to open your mind and your heart to the words on these pages, and to allow yourself to be transported to a world of emotion and reflection.

So, I offer this book to you, in the hope that it will provide a source of comfort, inspiration, and understanding as you navigate your own journey through life.

Acknowledgements

With deep gratitude, I acknowledge my grandfather, Late Shri NKP Singh, who has been my constant source of inspiration. This book would not have been possible without the support of my loving father Manish Ranjan Kumar, my mother Kalpana Devi, my sister Divya (Chulbuli), and my grandmother Krishna Devi. Their unwavering encouragement and belief in me has been the driving force behind my passion for writing. This book is dedicated to them, as a token of my love and appreciation.

Prologue

As you begin to delve into these pages, you will embark on a journey of self-discovery and reflection. This book is a collection of thoughts and experiences that have been woven together to create a tapestry of emotions and insights. Each verse and stanza captures a moment in time, a glimpse into the author's soul, and a celebration of life's beauty and complexities.

From the melancholic musings of a dying plant to the joy of observing the light of a loved one shining through a window at night, this book offers a glimpse into the many facets of the human experience. As you journey through these pages, we invite you to bring your own thoughts and emotions, to reflect on your own experiences, and to allow yourself to be transported to a place in between logic and fact.

So, take a deep breath, open your mind, and immerse yourself in the world of these poems. We hope that these words will inspire you, touch your heart, and leave a lasting impact on your soul.

1. In Memory of My Grandfather

Amidst the fields, where cows do graze,
With Grandpa, my childhood days.
Noon-time excursions we would make,
As he taught and I, with wonder, take.
Each day he'd return from office,
With a potli filled with dried fruit.
He'd whisper low, "Keep it just between us two,"
His love for me, forever true.
Alzheimer's came, took hold of his mind,
Our moments together, became harder to find.
I Was Sent to a hostel, tears I would shed,
But Grandpa's love, forever in my head.
Though he's gone, I still feel his embrace,
Memories of Grandpa, a warm and gentle place.
In my heart, his love doth live,
Forever shining, like a light that never wanes or shrive.

"So here's to you, my Grandpa,
Though you've passed away,
Your love and memory will always stand,
Forever and a day."

2. A Father's Joy

Today a child was born,
Filling the air with love and morn.
A bundle of joy, so small and sweet,
Bringing happiness to the father's feet.
His heart swells with pride,
As he gazes upon his newborn beside.
Tears of joy stream down his face,
As he takes in this wondrous grace.
He vows to love and protect,
To guide and support, with no neglect.
This child is his shining star,
Bringing joy to him, near and far.

"So here's to the father, strong and true,
Whose love for his child shines bright like the dew.
May this bond between them never cease,
Bringing endless happiness and peace."

3. Memories of the First

It starts with a shy smile,
A flutter of the heart,
A feeling so new and wild,
A love that sets us apart.
With every look, every touch,
Our hearts beat faster still,
As we surrender to this rush,
And let our love fulfill.
It's the first time we've felt this way,
With emotions so sincere,
As we bask in the light of day,
And bask in love so dear.
This love is like no other,
With a power pure and bright,
And it's with us now forever,
Guiding us through the night.
For in this moment, we know,
That our love will always grow,
With every passing day,
As we cherish it in every way.

4. Broken Dreams

It started with a crack,
A feeling of loss,
As the love that we once had,
Was suddenly lost.
The pain is so intense,
A wound that won't heal,
As we struggle with the sense,
Of love we can't steal.
We thought it would last,
This love that we found,
But now it's just a thing of the past,
And our hearts are on the ground.
The tears they never cease,
As we try to mend,
But the ache of heartbreak,
Won't come to an end.
It's the first time we've felt this pain,
Of love slipping away,
But we'll rise up again,
And love will come our way.
For heartbreak is just a part,
Of this journey we call life,
And in time, we'll mend our heart,
And love again with all our might.

5. A Winter Night's Reflection

The windows of the house at night,
Aglow with warm and yellow light,
They offer glimpses of a life,
That's cozy, safe, and free from strife.
I watch you from a distance, dear,
Not knowing that I'm standing near,
Your every move, your every laugh,
It all ignites a spark inside my heart.
The shadows stretch across the snow,
A tapestry of light and dark,
A scene of beauty, pure and slow,
That leaves my heart with a new spark.
But as much as I'd like to stay,
I must keep my distance and not give way,
For to reveal my love so true,
Would change the way you feel, I fear.
A once proud and verdant sight,
Now wilted, brown, and lifeless quite,
It stands alone, a mournful scene,
A symbol of what once has been.
The snow reflects the moonlight bright,
And adds a shimmer to the scene,

And I am left in a state of awe,
As I bask in this winter dream.
The night is filled with mystery,
Of shadows, love, and lost serenity,
And I am left with a feeling deep,
Of hope, regret, and memories to keep.

6. Between the Celestial Bars

Between the stars I roam with glee,
In this vast and endless sea,
Of shimmering lights, so bright and fair,
That dance and twirl without a care.
The air is filled with energy,
That flows through me like a melody,
And I am weightless, free, and light,
In this place that's full of delight.
I explore this realm with wonder,
And bask in its serene splendor,
With no bounds or limits to confine,
Only endless possibility and shine.
In between the stars I reside,
A part of something that's so wide,
And I bask in its serenity,
A being forever set free.
So here I'll stay, between the bars,
Of the celestial skies so vast,
Where I am free, without any scars,
And my spirit is forever fast.

7. Unrequited Love

It hit me like a stone,
The realization so clear,
That the love I had grown,
Was not returned, I fear.
My heart felt heavy and low,
As I faced this cruel fate,
Of loving someone who didn't know,
Or simply didn't appreciate.
The pain was so intense,
A wound that wouldn't heal,
As I struggled with the sense,
Of love that was not real.
The tears they wouldn't stop,
As I tried to make sense,
Of a love that wouldn't pop,
And a heart that wouldn't mend.
It was the first time I felt,
The pain of unrequited love,
But I learned to deal,
And rise above.
For not everyone we love,
Will love us back the same,
But we must find the strength,
To keep playing the game.

SATYAM RANJAN

8. A Heart in Pain

The day I made the choice,
To give up something I love,
Was also the day I felt lost,
My heart weighed down like a glove.
The pain of letting go,
Was more than I could bear,
As memories came and went,
Leaving me with such a scare.
Depression took hold,
Clouding my mind with its hue,
Making it hard to find the light,
And to see the good that's true.
But I know I must be strong,
And find my way through this strife,
For the future holds new hope,
And a chance to start a new life.
So I'll keep my head held high,
And fight the darkness with grace,
For I know that one day,
I'll see a brighter, happier place.

Reflections In The Twilight: An Epilogue

And so, we come to the end of this journey through windows and shadows. Through the pages of this book, we have explored the depths of our emotions and the beauty of the world around us. We have seen the light shining through windows in a house at night, the one we love unknowingly watched, the fragility of a dying plant, and the mystery of shadows on snow. Each poem has taken us on a unique journey, allowing us to see the world in a different light.

As we close this book, we take with us the memories of the words and images that have touched our hearts. May they continue to inspire us and bring us comfort as we face the challenges of life.

And so, we remember the late Shri NKP Singh, the grandfather of the author, who has always been a source of love and inspiration in their life. May his memory continue to live on through the pages of this book.

We would like to express our gratitude to our father Manish Ranjan Kumar, mother Kalpana Devi, sister Divya (Chulbuli), and grandmother Krishna Devi for their constant love and support. Without their encouragement and guidance, this book would not have been possible.

Contact the Author: You can contact Satyam Ranjan via email at **Satyamsingh2306@gmail.com**

Follow the Author: You can follow Satyam Ranjan on social media platforms such as

- Twitter (Satyam_Ranjann)
- Instagram (satyam_ranjan)
- Linkedin (satyamranjan)
- Youtube (Satyam Ranjan)

- Google (Satyam Ranjan)

We hope you enjoyed the book and that it provided you with a deeper understanding of yourself and the world around you. If you did enjoy the book, please consider leaving a review on Amazon, Goodreads or any other book review site. Your support will help other readers to discover this book and the author's work.

Printed by Libri Plureos GmbH in Hamburg,
Germany